CYCLING

A TRUE BOOK

by

Christin Ditchfield

Children's Press®
A Division of Grolier Publishing
New York London Hong Kong Sydney
Danbury, Connecticut

BMX cyclist doing a
one-handed jump

Reading Consultant
Linda Cornwell
*Coordinator of School Quality
and Professional Improvement
Indiana State Teachers
Association*

Cycling Consultant
Jordan Grauer
*Professional
Competitive Cyclist*

Note to the reader:
*In the world of cycling, the metric
system is used to measure dis-
tances. Here's a metric-conversion
website you can visit to help you
convert kilometers to miles:*
http://tqjunior.advanced.org/3804

**Visit Children's Press® on
the Internet at:
http://publishing.grolier.com**

Library of Congress Cataloging-in-Publication Data

Ditchfield, Christin.
    Cycling / by Christin Ditchfield.
        p.   cm. — (A true book)
    Includes bibliographical references (p.   ) and index.
    Summary: Describes the history, equipment, techniques, and competi-
tions of the sport of cycling.
    ISBN 0-516-21061-0 (lib. bdg.)   0-516-27024-9 (pbk.)
    1. Cycling Juvenile literature. [1. Bicycles and bicycling.] I. Title.
II. Series.
GV1043.5.D58 2000
796.6—dc21   99-28190
                                                                    CIP
                                                                    AC

© 2000 by Children's Press®,
A Division of Grolier Publishing Co., Inc.
All rights reserved. Published simultaneously in Canada.
Printed in the United States of America.
1 2 3 4 5 6 7 8 9 0 R 09 08 07 06 05 04 03 02 01 00

Contents

A Draisienne of 1818

How It All Began

In 1839, a Scottish blacksmith came up with a great idea. Kirkpatrick Macmillan decided to attach pedals to his Draisienne—a scooterlike machine that had two big wheels. He had invented the bicycle. This vehicle, however, never really caught on.

Other people had similar ideas. Each one tried to create a better machine. The first bicycle to become popular was invented in 1861 by two French men, Pierre Michaux and his son Ernest. The frame of their bicycle was made of iron, and the wheels were made of wood. It was heavy and not very comfortable. People sometimes called this bicycle the "bone-shaker" because of its bumpy ride.

Man riding a "bone-shaker" (left)
and bicycles of the 1890s (right)

Inventors kept experimenting
with different styles and materials. As the machines improved,
cycling quickly became popular
all over the world.

People enjoyed riding bikes
for fun and exercise. They

Bicycling became a popular form of exercise in the early 1900s.

found that bicycles provided simple and inexpensive transportation. And of course, bicycling turned out to be a great sport!

In 1868, the first official bicycle race took place, in

The start of a bicycle race in the late 1800s

Paris, France. Bicycle races were even included in the first modern Olympics, in 1896.

Since then, competitive cycling has become an intense athletic sport. Cyclists train hard to be in top physical condition. They ride scientifically

Today, competitive
cycling is an intense,
exciting sport.

designed machines built from
the same materials as jet planes
and bulletproof vests. Cyclists
compete in a wide variety of
races and events. The sport
has come a long way.

The Equipment

Cyclists use special equipment to give them the winning edge. Most of this equipment is designed to increase speed.

When cyclists move forward, the air resists them and slows them down. This slowing effect is called aerodynamic drag. To reduce the drag,

cyclists keep everything
simple and streamlined.

Competitive cyclists ride
"low-profile" bicycles—light,
thin bikes with low handlebars. These handlebars
decrease wind resistance by
letting the rider lean over the

To gain as much speed as possible, cyclists ride low-profile bikes and wear streamlined clothing.

front of the bike. For some cycling events, cyclists use bikes that have disc-wheels in the back. The flat surface of the disc reduces the drag that affects ordinary spoke wheels.

A racing bike should be strong, but not heavy. Frames are usually made from such lightweight materials as steel, aluminum, carbon fiber, or titanium.

A cyclist's clothes are designed for speed as well as safety. Competitors wear skin-tight racing outfits and special shoes, gloves, and glasses.

Cycling shoes have stiff soles. The cleats on the bottom of the shoes help the rider's feet stay on the pedals. Gloves absorb vibrations from the road, and glasses shield the eyes from dirt and dust, as

A cyclist's clothes are designed for both speed and safety. Competitive cyclists wear special helmets, gloves, and shoes.

well as from the sun. A light-weight helmet protects the cyclist's head.

It takes great strength and energy to compete in bicycle races. Cyclists know it is important to eat healthy foods and get plenty of rest. Many cyclists lift weights and train at a gym to improve their fitness levels. Coaches work with cyclists to teach them the skills and techniques they will need in competition.

Bicycle Basics

These are the major parts of a bicycle:

handlebars

seat or saddle

frame

spokes

rim

brakes

wheels

pedals

gears

chain

The Races

Bicycle races can be divided into two categories—road races and track races.

Road races are usually 40 to 250 kilometers long. These races take place on the streets of a city or on roads between nearby towns. The course is measured and marked out

Road races often involve hundreds of cyclists.

ahead of time. Spectators line up along the road to watch the action.

In road races, hundreds of cyclists can compete at the

In road races, cyclists ride together in a group called a peloton.

same time. The cyclists ride together in a main group called a peloton. When the riders stay close to one another, there is less aerodynamic drag.

The person in the front of the group gets most of the wind resistance. It's hard work for that cyclist to keep pushing for-ward, but it makes it easier for everyone behind that person.

The lead cyclist in a road race gets most of the wind resistance.

Cyclists often race in teams, so team members help each other by taking turns in the front. Near the end of the course, the strongest riders break away from the group and race to the finish.

Track races take place on an oval-shaped track called a velodrome. A velodrome may be in an indoor or outdoor arena. The track is made of concrete or wood, and the corners of the track have steep slopes.

Track races take place on a velodrome.

Several kinds of races are held
on a velodrome, including
sprints, pursuits, points races,
and a 1-kilometer time trial.
　　In the time trial, each
cyclist races alone against

A sprint race (above) and a team pursuit race (right)

the clock. Sprints are short races between two riders. In pursuits, riders start on opposite sides of the track and chase each other for a given distance. If neither rider catches his opponent, the race goes the full distance. The winner is whoever covers the given distance in the shortest time.

Points races require cyclists to ride many laps around the velodrome. Different parts of the race are timed, and riders score points for their position during those segments.

The Tour de France

The Tour de France is the most prestigious professional road race in the world. The cyclists ride about 4,000 kilometers through western Europe in a race that takes three weeks to complete.

The length of the race makes it a grueling competition. Day

The Tour de France takes three weeks to complete as cyclists race across the French countryside (above) and into the city of Paris (right).

after day, the cyclists must push themselves to compete against the world's best riders.

Each day of the Tour de France, the cyclist who is in first place gets to wear the *maillot jaune*—the yellow jersey.

At night, the athletes try to get as much rest as they can before the next day's race.

The race is divided into sections, called stages. Different riders may win different stages. Each day, the cyclist with the lowest overall time gets to wear the *maillot jaune*—the yellow jersey. When all the stages have been completed, the victory and the yellow jersey belong to the cyclist with the best overall time.

A Tour de France champion

Guts and Glory

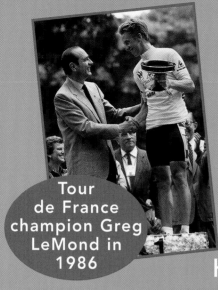

Tour de France champion Greg LeMond in 1986

In 1986, Greg LeMond became the first American—and the first non-European—to win the Tour de France. Soon after his victory, Greg was badly injured in a hunting accident. Doctors weren't sure he would ever walk again, let alone race. His career seemed finished. But LeMond refused to quit. He battled his way back to the top of his sport. Greg LeMond won the Tour de France again in 1989 and 1990.

LeMond recovering from his accident

LeMond competing in the 1990 Tour de France

LeMond celebrating his 1990 Tour de France win

The Olympics

Cycling has been a part of the modern Olympic Games since the beginning. Three bicycle races were included in the 1896 Olympic Games in Athens, Greece. A French man named Paul Masson won two of them. Over the years, the Olympic Committee has added more cycling races to the games.

French cyclist Paul Masson (above, at right) won two gold medals at the 1896 Olympic Games. Women's cycling (left) has been part of the Olympics since 1984.

Until recently, all these events were for men. Women competed in Olympic cycling events for the first time at the 1984 Olympics in Los Angeles. Connie Carpenter Phinney, an American, won the first gold medal given for women's cycling.

Today, the men's competition includes the following track events: kilometer time trial, sprint, pursuit, team pursuit, and points race.

A men's Olympic
road race

Road events include time
trial, team time trial, and road
race. Women's competitions
include the sprint, the individ-
ual pursuit, and road races.

New Cycling Sports

Many new cycling sports have been invented in recent years. Mountain biking has become extremely popular. Mountain bikes ride "off-road"—that is, up hills, across fields, and through forests. Their bikes are specially designed to stand up to rough conditions.

Mountain bikes have knobby tires for better traction.

Mountain bikes have sturdy frames and wide, knobby tires with deep tread for better traction. Mountain bikes also have extra gears for control.

A mountain biker needs good balance to stay on the bike as it bumps over rocks, roots, and other obstacles. The biker must also learn how to steer and brake well.

Mountain bikers riding through a stream

A mountain bike competition usually includes downhill and cross-country races. In downhill races, mountain bikers wear a lot of protective gear—

Mountain bikers wear a lot of protective gear during downhill races.

helmets, goggles, face guards, chest protectors, and arm and leg pads. Cross-country mountain-bike racing has been an Olympic-medal sport since 1996.

Another popular cycling sport is BMX racing. The letters "BMX" stand for "bicycle motocross." In freestyle events, cyclists perform wheelies, jumps, and other tricks. During a BMX race, the cyclists compete on a dirt

A BMX
freestyle
event (above)
and a BMX
race (left)

track that has many twists, turns, and bumps. BMX racers spend much of the time flying through the air on their bikes!

Although BMX bikes are small and light, they are also very sturdy. They must be strong enough to withstand rough landings. Because of the speed and the jumping, BMX bikers sometimes fall off their bikes. Often, the bikers collide with other racers. So

BMX bikers
sometimes fall
off their bikes.

BMX bikers, like mountain bikers, wear a lot of protective clothing. This type of racing may be dangerous, but it's also very exciting!

Cyclocross

Cyclocross is a sport for cyclists who like challenges. Athletes compete in this off-road event during the cold and rainy winter months. They ride around rocks and tree stumps just like mountain bikers. But on a cyclocross course, there are some things you can't maneuver around, such as fences, streams, and steep hills. To get past these obstacles, the cyclist gets off his bike and carries it on his shoulders while he runs—quickly, of course. The fastest person wins the race!

To Find Out More

Here are some additional resources to help you learn more about cycling:

 **Books**

Gutman, Bill. **BMX Racing.** Capstone Press, 1995.

Jensen, Julie. **Beginning Mountain Biking.** Lerner Publishing Co., 1997.

Kent, Jessica. **Racing Bikes.** EDC Publications, 1991.

Lord, Trevor. **Amazing Bikes.** Alfred A. Knopf, Inc., 1992.

Thomas, Ron, and Herran, Joe. **The Grolier Student Encyclopedia of the Olympic Games.** Grolier Educational, 1996.

Organizations and Online Sites

BMXtra Online Magazine
http://www.bmxtra.com/

Photos and information about BMX racing.

United States Olympic Committee (USOC)
Olympic House
One Olympic Plaza
Colorado Springs, CO
80909-5760
http://www.usoc.org

The United States Olympic Committee supervises Olympic activity for the United States. Its website includes everything you want to know about Olympic sports, past and present.

USA Cycling, Inc.
One Olympic Plaza
Colorado Springs, CO
80909
http://www.usacycling.org

Includes the latest news about cycling, calenders of cycling events, and information on all types of bike racing.

Velo News Interactive
http://www.velonew.com

This site contains everything you ever wanted to know about professional cycling.

Important Words

aerodynamic drag slowing effect of air on the body and the bicycle

disc wheel wheel with a flat surface instead of spokes

frame basic metal structure of a bicycle

gears system of controls that makes pedaling easier or harder

maneuver move skillfully

overall including everything

peloton French word for group, pack, or bunch

resists works against

streamline to make something more simple and efficient

traction friction that keeps tires from slipping on a surface

Index

Meet the Author

Christin Ditchfield is the author of several books for Children's Press, including five True Books on Summer Olympic sports. Her interviews with celebrity athletes have appeared in magazines all over the world. Ms. Ditchfield makes her home in Sarasota, Florida.